Can I Retire?

How Much Money You Need to Retire and
How to Manage Your Retirement Savings,
Explained in 100 Pages or Less

Can I Retire?

How Much Money You Need to Retire and
How to Manage Your Retirement Savings,
Explained in 100 Pages or Less

Mike Piper, CPA

Why is there a light bulb on the cover?

In cartoons and comics, a light bulb is often used to signify a moment of clarity or sudden understanding—an "aha!" moment. My hope is that the books in the *"...in 100 pages or less"* series can help readers achieve clarity and understanding of topics that are often considered complex and confusing—hence the light bulb.

Dedication

To every investor navigating his or her way through the morass of market uncertainty, tax complexity, and conflicting advice.

Disclaimer

This book is not intended to be a substitute for personalized advice from a professional accountant or attorney. Nothing contained within this text should be construed as tax advice. The publisher and author make no representation or warranty as to this book's adequacy or appropriateness for any purpose. Similarly, no representation or warranty is made as to the accuracy of the material in this book.

Purchasing this book does not create any client relationship or other advisory, fiduciary, or professional services relationship with the publisher or with the author. *You alone* bear the *sole* responsibility of assessing the merits and risks associated with any financial decisions you make. And it should always be kept in mind that any investment can result in partial or complete loss.

Your Feedback is Appreciated!

As the author of this book, I'm very interested to hear your thoughts. If you find the book helpful, please let me know! Alternatively, if you have any suggestions of ways to make the book better, I'm eager to hear that, too.

Finally, if you're unhappy with your purchase for any reason, let me know, and I'll be happy to provide you with a refund of the current list price of the book (limited to one refund per household per title).

You can reach me at: mike@simplesubjects.com.

Best Regards,
Mike Piper, CPA

Table of Contents

INTRODUCTION

Time to Make a Plan

There are already several excellent books about retirement planning. For example, *The Bogleheads' Guide to Retirement Planning* is a wonderful resource, as is Michael Zwecher's *Retirement Portfolios*.

So why did I decide to write another? How does this book hope to be better than all of those other books?

It doesn't. *Can I Retire?* is not intended to be better. It's intended to be shorter. It's written for the person who might not be able to find the time to read a lengthier book.

If you're considering reading a more in-depth guide to retirement planning, I wholeheartedly encourage you to do so. But if there's a good chance that, if you were to buy one of those other books, it would sit unread on your coffee table or bookshelf, then this book is written for you.

Retirement Planning: Create a Plan!

The goal of retirement planning is to create a plan. It feels silly to come out and say that, but most people never actually take the step of creating a specific plan. Instead, they read a handful of articles about various retirement planning topics, they spend a little time doing a few rough calculations, and then they make a mostly-blind leap into retirement.

The more specifically you've planned how you'll manage your portfolio—and your finances in general—the less likely it is that you'll have to go back to work or dramatically reduce your spending later in retirement.

Of course, a retirement plan isn't set in stone. Unexpected expenses come up, tax laws change, and investment returns are unpredictable. But having a concrete, well-thought-out plan will help you:

- Reduce the likelihood of investment mistakes, such as panicking and selling an investment at the wrong time,
- Avoid wasting money on taxes simply because you're unaware of the tax-saving strategies available to you, and
- Prepare your nest egg to withstand a myriad of risks including poor investment returns, inflation, and the possibility that you'll live far longer than you had expected.

What This Book Will Cover

This book is intended to help you answer two questions as a part of your retirement planning process:

1. How much money do I need saved before I can retire?
2. Once I am retired, how should I manage my savings to minimize the risk of outliving my money?

Naturally, we'll break both of those questions down into several important sub-topics. But as you can see, there are still many retirement planning issues that this book *won't* cover—things like whether or not you should buy long-term care insurance, what to look for in an LTC policy, when to begin taking Social Security benefits, when your spouse should begin taking benefits, and so on.

As such, I suggest supplementing the information you gain from this book with either:

- The services of a trustworthy, unbiased, well-informed financial planner, or
- An ongoing program of self-education, should you decide to handle your own financial planning.

PART ONE

How Much Money Will I Need to Retire?

CHAPTER ONE

How Much Income Do You Need?

It all starts with that question. There's really no way around it.

If you want, you can cheat by using a popular rule of thumb such as, "In retirement, you'll need 75% of your pre-retirement income." But who can say whether that rule of thumb will actually hold true *for you*? Different people have different plans for retirement, and it's common sense that those different plans come with different price tags.

In short, unless you're comfortable with the idea of looking for work several years into retirement, there's no viable alternative to sitting down and calculating how much income *you* are going to need.

Calculating Your Expenses

Fortunately, such calculations aren't as difficult as you might think. A simple two-step process can get the job done:

1. Determine your current expenses.
2. Do your best to estimate how those expenses will change.

To get the most meaningful figure of your current expenses, be sure to look at the last full year rather than just the last few months. Yes, it's more work, but it prevents you from overlooking expenses that you only pay once per year, such as certain insurance premiums or annual vacations.

To calculate your expenses over the last year, you'll need three things: credit card statements, bank statements, and your payroll stubs (for expenses like insurance that were deducted directly from your wages).

After tallying up your expenses for the last year, do your best to adjust for things that will change in retirement. For example:

- Saving for retirement: You won't need to do it anymore once you're retired.
- Mortgage payment: If it hasn't already, this will go away once you've paid off your mortgage completely.

- Work-related expenses (dry cleaning and commuting costs, for instance) will mostly disappear.
- Health insurance premiums: How will they change as you age, as you become ineligible for your plan at work, and as you become eligible for Medicare?
- Entertainment costs: Do you plan to travel the world, or do you anticipate spending time on a hobby that might even earn money?

Of course, most of the figures here will be estimates. That's OK. You don't need a precise, to-the-penny budget. Any estimate based on your own goals and needs is going to be more accurate than the amount recommended by a rule of thumb.

Adjusting for Inflation

If you're many years away from retirement, it's important to revisit this spending-tracking exercise on a regular basis (every 2-3 years, for instance). That way, your planning figures will be updated to account for both inflation and lifestyle changes that have occurred in the interim.

Adjusting for Taxes

Of course, due to taxes, in order to cover a given amount of annual expenses, you're going to need a greater dollar amount of annual income.

EXAMPLE: Larry expects his annual retirement expenses to be around $40,000. Between state and federal taxes, he expects to pay a combined average tax rate in retirement of 10%. In order to cover his expenses, he'll need $44,444 of pre-tax income, calculated as $40,000 ÷ 0.9 (because 90% of his pre-tax income is what will be available to spend, given a 10% average tax rate).

Pensions, Social Security, and Other Income

When determining whether you've saved enough in order to retire, the goal isn't to determine how much income you need each year, but rather how much income you need each year *from your investments*. To arrive at that figure, subtract any other income that you expect to receive—Social Security benefits, pension income, a part-time job, etc.

For example, if you expect to need $45,000 of pre-tax income each year, and you expect to receive a total of $20,000 from Social Security and pension income, you only need to fund $25,000 each year with your savings.[1]

To view an estimate of the Social Security benefit you can expect to receive, you can create an account on the Social Security Administration website (ssa.gov/myaccount).

Social Security planning strategies are beyond the scope of this book, but it's worth pointing out that the decision of when to start taking Social Security benefits is one worthy of serious consideration. Depending on your circumstances, it may be best to start taking benefits as soon as you're eligible, or it may be best to wait as long as you can. Or, it may be beneficial to use more advanced strategies such as claiming spousal benefits upon reaching your "full retirement age" while waiting until age 70 to claim your own retirement benefit.

The Social Security claiming decision is covered in more depth in my book *Social Security Made Simple*.

---

[1] Remember, if you have a pension that isn't adjusted for inflation, it will satisfy a smaller and smaller portion of your needs each year—thereby increasing the amount you'll need to fund with your investments.

Chapter 1 Simple Summary

- The first step to retirement planning is to estimate how much income you'll need per year in retirement.

- When calculating your annual expenses, be sure to use an entire year of data so that you don't miss any expenses that are only paid once per year.

- Remember to account for income taxes when calculating how much income you'll need from your portfolio.

- When calculating the income you'll need from your portfolio, remember to subtract any income you expect to receive from other sources—pensions, Social Security, etc.

- As you get closer and closer to retirement, it's worth revisiting these calculations. A tabulation of your expenses one year prior to retirement will be much more useful than data from ten years prior to retirement.

CHAPTER TWO

Safe Withdrawal Rates: The 4% "Rule"

After determining how much income you need your investments to provide each year, the next question is: How much savings will it take to provide the desired level of income?

The most commonly-given answer to this question involves yet another rule of thumb: the 4% rule. This guideline comes from research done in 1994 by financial advisor William Bengen (and an assortment of follow-up research by various parties in the decades since), which found that if you plan to increase the amount you withdraw from your portfolio each year in order to keep up with inflation, the most you can withdraw from your portfolio in the first year of a thirty-year retirement is 4%, unless you want to run a significant risk of running out of money.

EXAMPLE: Susan retires with a $600,000 portfolio. According to the 4% rule, she should be able to withdraw $24,000 from the portfolio in her first year of retirement, and increase her withdrawal each year in keeping with inflation.

Why Only 4%?

Given that the U.S. stock market has averaged an inflation-adjusted return of just over 7% from 1926-2017, many people are surprised at such a low suggested withdrawal rate. If the stock market averages a 7% return, why can't somebody with a portfolio of stocks or stock mutual funds plan to spend 7% per year? There are two reasons, and they're both related to the unpredictability of investment returns.

Volatility Is Bad News When Selling.

You've likely read about the virtues of dollar-cost-averaging (that is, making systematic purchases of an investment). The idea is that if you purchase a fixed dollar amount of a stock or mutual fund every month, you'll be buying more shares when the stock's price is low and fewer when it's high. In other words, you'll be automating the "buy low" part of the old adage to "buy low, sell high."

In retirement, however, the opposite is true. When you're retired, you're systematically *selling* your holdings rather than buying more. And if you're dollar-cost-averaging *out* of a volatile investment, you'll be selling more shares when the price is low and fewer shares when the price is high. This is not a good thing.

The takeaway here is that once you begin liquidating your investments, volatility takes on a whole new significance: It directly reduces your returns. So even if the stock market earns a specific return over the course of your retirement, it's likely that your own stock portfolio (even if it's held in index funds that track the market) will earn a lesser return due to the return-damaging effect of dollar-cost-averaging *out* of a volatile investment.

Sequence of Returns Risk (a.k.a. "Luck")

"Sequence of returns risk" is the second reason that it's not safe to withdraw 7% per year even if you expect your portfolio to earn an average return of 7% per year throughout your retirement. It's a fancy term, but all it really means is this: The *order* in which returns occur matters a great deal.

Specifically, when you're systematically taking money *out* of an investment portfolio, the early returns (i.e., the ones that occur while you still have a lot of money invested) are the ones that matter most.

If you're withdrawing more than a few percent of your portfolio per year, and you experience a severe or extended bear market early in retirement, there might not be enough of your portfolio left for your retirement to be saved when the market finally does rebound.

EXAMPLE: Agnes retires with a $400,000 portfolio, from which she takes $15,000 at the beginning of each year. Over the first five years of her retirement, her portfolio earns the following annual returns: 15%, 12%, 3%, -6%, -12%.

Her portfolio values at the end of each year will be as follows:

- Year 1: $442,750
- Year 2: $479,080
- Year 3: $478,002
- Year 4: $435,222
- Year 5: $369,796.

If, however, the returns had occurred in the opposite order, her portfolio value would look as follows:

- Year 1: $338,800
- Year 2: $304,372
- Year 3: $298,053
- Year 4: $317,020
- Year 5: $347,322

That's a difference of more than $22,000 in ending value—just because the returns occurred in a different *order.* As you'll note, the scenario in which the good returns occurred first turned out better for Agnes. That's because, when you're withdrawing money, the earlier returns have a greater impact than the later returns.

To see how big an effect the sequence of returns can have over the course of your retirement, imagine the case of an investor who retires with a $500,000 portfolio, invested 50% in stocks, 50% in bonds, and rebalanced annually. She uses a starting annual withdrawal rate of 6% (i.e., $30,000), which she then adjusts upward to keep up with inflation.

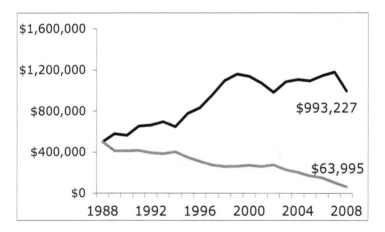

The top line shows what would have happened if the investor retired at the end of 1988, right before the roaring bull market of the 1990s. Twenty years into her retirement, her portfolio value would have nearly doubled to $993,227.

But what's that line at the bottom? That line indicates what would have happened if those twenty years of returns (and inflation) had occurred in the opposite order. In that scenario, the investor's portfolio has declined to just $63,995, and will very likely be depleted within the next two years (especially given that the inflation-adjusted annual withdrawal has by this point grown to more than $50,000).

That's a huge difference! Twenty years into retirement, you could be a millionaire, or rapidly approaching broke, depending solely upon the *order* in which your investment returns occur—something over which you have no control. This is, in part, why it's generally wise to use a conservative withdrawal rate. You don't want to risk depleting your portfolio simply due to an unlucky order of returns.

It's Only a Guideline.

Like any rule of thumb, the 4% rule isn't a hard-and-fast rule, so much as a rough guideline. The original study didn't account for retirements that last longer than 30 years, so if a lengthier retirement is a possibility for you, it would be wise to consider a starting withdrawal rate below 4%. In addition, the study assumes that you won't make any investing mistakes, such as panicking and selling during a crash or picking a mutual fund that underperforms the market.

And, as with any guideline based on historical investment returns, it's only useful to the extent that future returns mimic past returns. And there's no guarantee that they will. With the stock portion of your portfolio, there's simply no way to know what type of returns you're likely to get over those first few crucial years at the beginning of your retirement. With the bond portion of your portfolio, things are somewhat more predictable due to the fact that today's bond yields serve as a reasonably good estimate for expected returns in the near future. For example, as of this writing, bond yields are significantly below their historical averages, which suggests that it might be wise to use a withdrawal rate that's lower than what would have worked in the past.

It's also worth noting that the 4% rule makes a somewhat unrealistic assumption about the way in which people spend from their portfolios. It assumes that people spend the same amount (adjusted for inflation) from their portfolio each year, regardless of circumstances. In reality, most people adjust their spending based on how well or how poorly their portfolio has performed. For example, if your portfolio performs poorly during the first few years of your retirement, if you are like most people, you will reduce your rate of spending, rather than blithely continuing to spend at the same pace, despite your dwindling portfolio balance. Relative to a strategy of fixed (inflation-adjusted) spending, a strategy in which you adjust spending slightly each year based on portfolio performance both makes you safer (because you reduce your spending if things go poorly) and, on average, allows you to spend somewhat more over time (because you adjust spending upward slightly if your portfolio is consistently growing).

Chapter 2 Simple Summary

- 4% is typically thought to be the highest starting withdrawal rate that you can use for a 30-year retirement, unless you want to run a significant risk of outliving your savings.

- Because of the negative effects of volatility and sequence of returns risk, it's important to use a starting withdrawal rate that's *lower* than the inflation-adjusted return you expect to earn on your portfolio.

- The 4% "rule" is only a historical guideline. There's no guarantee that it will work.

- Adjusting spending slightly over time based on portfolio performance reduces the probability of depleting your portfolio and, on average, allows you to spend more over the course of your retirement.

CHAPTER THREE

What if 4% Isn't Enough?

In order to retire with a 4% withdrawal rate, your retirement portfolio must be 25-times your annual pre-tax income needs. So if you need, for example, $35,000 of pre-tax income from your investments, you'd need to save $875,000 before you can retire. (And as we mentioned in the previous chapter, there's no guarantee that even a 4% withdrawal rate is low enough to be safe.)

Unfortunately, for many investors nearing retirement age, saving 25-times their necessary investment income just isn't going to happen. They're too close to retirement—and too far away from that goal—for it to be possible.

If you're in such a situation, there are five primary options for getting your retirement savings to where they need to be:

1. Cut your expenses now (so you can save more each year),
2. Cut your planned expenses in retirement,

3. Work part-time during retirement,
4. Retire later than you originally planned, or
5. Annuitize a portion of your portfolio.[1]

Each of these methods *will* get you closer to the amount of money necessary for retiring safely. But they all involve making sacrifices, and that's never popular. As a result, many people try to create an option #6: aim for higher investment returns so that your portfolio will grow faster between now and retirement.

Increasing Returns is No Easy Task.

The most common approaches to seeking higher returns are to:

1. Include a heavier stock allocation in your portfolio, or
2. Attempt to outperform the market.

Increasing your stock allocation in an attempt to increase returns might work. Or, it might not. While stocks have historically earned greater returns than bonds, there's absolutely no guarantee that they'll outperform bonds (or earn a positive return at all, for that matter) over any particular

---

[1] Using annuities to achieve a higher withdrawal rate is the subject of the next chapter.

period. Moving more of your money into stocks shortly before retirement is a risky strategy.

Similarly, attempting to earn above-market returns has the potential to backfire. It's not impossible, but it's one heck of a feat to be able to do it reliably. In fact, even the pros can't seem to get the job done consistently. According to a study done by Standard and Poors, for the ten-year period ending 6/30/2017, less than 15% of U.S. stock mutual funds and less than 21% of international stock funds managed to outperform their respective benchmarks.[1] And that's not a fluke. Standard and Poors has been doing this study for years, and it consistently shows the same thing: Even the professionals have less than a 50% chance of beating the stock market.[2]

If you have no reason to think that you have a meaningful advantage over the professionals—and I would argue that most investors do not—then the only reliable answer is to adjust your plans. Figure out a way to make your retirement work without earning superstar investment returns, whether that means retiring later, working part-time in retirement, cutting your expenses, or (as we'll discuss next) annuitizing a part of your portfolio.

---

[1] The study is available at:
http://us.spindices.com/spiva/#/reports
[2] This is why I advocate investing via low-cost index funds that seek only to *match* the market's return. We'll discuss that topic a bit more in Chapter 7.

Chapter 3 Simple Summary

- If a 4% withdrawal rate isn't high enough to satisfy your goals, your best bet is to cut your spending or postpone retirement.

- Increasing your stock allocation in an attempt to earn higher returns can backfire. Stock returns are simply not predictable over any particular period.

- Reliably earning above-market returns is extremely difficult. Attempting to do so involves taking on a significant risk of *under*performing the market.

CHAPTER FOUR

Retirement Planning with Annuities

Many annuities (maybe even most) are a raw deal for investors. They carry needlessly high expenses and surrender charges, and their contracts are so complex that very few investors can properly assess whether the annuity is a good investment.

That said, one specific type of annuity can be an extremely useful tool for retirement planning: the single premium immediate annuity (SPIA).

What's a SPIA?

A single premium immediate annuity is a contract with an insurance company whereby:

1. You pay them a sum of money up front (known as a premium), and

2. They promise to pay you a certain amount of money periodically (monthly, for instance) for the rest of your life.[1]

A single premium immediate annuity can be a fixed annuity or a variable annuity. With a single premium immediate *fixed* annuity, the payout is a fixed amount each period. With a single premium immediate *variable* annuity, the payout is linked to the performance of a mutual fund. For the most part, I'd suggest steering clear of variable annuities. They tend to be complex and expensive. And because they each offer different bells and whistles, it's difficult to make comparisons between annuity providers to see which one offers the best deal.

In contrast, fixed SPIAs are helpful tools for two reasons:

1. They make retirement planning easier, and
2. They allow for a higher withdrawal rate than you can *safely* take from a portfolio of stocks, bonds, and mutual funds over the course of a potentially-lengthy retirement.

It's also possible to buy a fixed SPIA with a payout that adjusts upward each year in keeping with inflation. Naturally, inflation-adjusted fixed annuities

---

[1] There are also some SPIAs that only pay out for a fixed period, rather than for the rest of your life. However, for the purposes of this book, when I use the term SPIA, I'm referring to a lifetime annuity.

require higher initial premiums than fixed annuities without an inflation adjustment.

Retirement Planning with SPIAs

Fixed SPIAs make retirement planning easier in exactly the same way that traditional pensions do: They're predictable. If you know that you need $X of income each year in retirement, you can go to an online annuity quote provider, put in $X as the payout, check "yes" for inflation adjustments, and you'll get an answer: "For $Y, you can purchase an annuity that will pay you $X per year, adjusted for inflation, for the rest of your life—no matter how long you might live."[1]

Pretty easy, right? You now have a specific figure for the minimum amount of savings necessary to retire safely. With a traditional stock and bond portfolio, retirement planning is more of a guessing game.

---

[1] In order to get the most meaningful figure, be sure to get a quote for a SPIA with a payout linked to the consumer price index, rather than one that simply promises a fixed percentage increase from year to year.

SPIAs and Withdrawal Rates

Fixed SPIAs are also helpful because they allow you to retire on less money than you would need with a typical stock/bond portfolio. For example, even with the low interest rates that prevail as of this writing, according to immediateannuities.com (a website that provides annuity quotes from various insurance companies), a 65-year-old male could purchase an inflation-indexed annuity paying 4.7% annually.

If that investor were to take a withdrawal rate of 4.7% from a typical stock/bond portfolio, then adjust the withdrawal upward each year for inflation, there's a meaningful chance that he'd run out of money during his lifetime—especially given the current environment of low interest rates and high stock valuations. That risk disappears with an annuity.

How is that possible? In short, it's possible because the annuitant gives up the right to keep the money once he dies. If you buy a SPIA and die the next day, the money is gone.[1] Your heirs don't get to keep it—the insurance company does. And the insurance company uses (most of) that money to fund

---

[1] There are some exceptions. For example, you can buy a SPIA that promises to pay income for the *longer* of your lifetime or a given number of years. But purchasing such an add-on reduces the payout, thereby reducing the ability of the SPIA to do what it does so well—provide a relatively high payout with very little risk.

the payouts on SPIAs purchased by people who are still living.

In essence, SPIA purchasers who die before reaching their life expectancy end up funding the retirement of SPIA purchasers who live past their life expectancy.

But I Want to Leave Something to My Heirs!

For many people, it's a deal-breaker to learn that none of the money used to purchase an annuity will go to their heirs.

The relevant counterpoint here is that, depending on how your desired level of spending compares to the size of your portfolio, choosing not to devote any portion of your portfolio to an annuity could backfire. That is, there's a possibility that, rather than resulting in a larger inheritance for your kids, the decision results in you running out of money while you're still alive, thereby causing you to become a financial burden on your kids.

Annuity Income: Is It Safe?

Because the income from an annuity is backed by an insurance company, financial advisors and financial literature usually refer to it as "guaranteed." But that doesn't mean it's a 100% sure-thing. Just like any company, insurance companies can go belly-up. It's not common, but it's certainly not impossible, especially given that:

1. The longer the period in question, the greater the likelihood of any given company going out of business, and
2. The entire point of a lifetime annuity is to protect you against longevity risk (that is, the risk that you last longer than your money). So presumably, we're talking about a fairly long period of time.

However, if you're careful, the possibility of your annuity provider going out of business doesn't have to keep you up at night.

Check Your Insurance Company's Financial Strength

Before placing a meaningful portion of your retirement savings in the hands of an insurance company, it's important to check that company's financial strength. I'd suggest checking with multiple ratings agencies, such as Standard and Poor's, Moody's, or A.M. Best. (Note that each of these companies uses a different ratings scale, so it's important to look at what each of the ratings actually means.)

State Guaranty Associations

Even if the issuer of your annuity *does* go bankrupt, you aren't necessarily in trouble. Each state has a guaranty association (funded by the insurance companies themselves) that will step in if your insurance company goes insolvent.

It's important to note, however, that the state guaranty associations only provide coverage up to a certain limit. And that limit varies from state to state. Equally important: The rules regarding the coverage vary from state to state.

For example, the guaranty association in Connecticut provides coverage of up to $500,000 per contract owner, per insurance company insolvency. But they only provide coverage to investors who are residents of Connecticut at the time the insurance company becomes insolvent. So if you have an annuity currently worth $500,000, and you move to Arkansas (where the coverage is capped at $300,000), you're putting your money at risk.

In contrast, the guaranty association in New York offers $500,000 of coverage, and they cover you if you are a NY state resident either when the insurance company goes insolvent *or* when the annuity was issued. So moving to another state with a lower coverage limit isn't a problem if you bought your annuity in New York.

Minimizing Your Risk

In short, annuities can be a very useful tool for minimizing the risk that you'll run out of money in retirement. But to maximize the likelihood that you'll receive the promised payout, it's important to take the following steps:

1. Check the financial strength of the insurance company before purchasing an annuity.
2. Know the limit for guaranty association coverage in your state as well as the rules accompanying such coverage.
3. Consider diversifying between insurance companies. For instance, if your state's guaranty association only provides coverage up to $250,000 and you want to annuitize $400,000 of your portfolio, consider buying a $200,000 annuity from each of two different insurance companies.
4. Before moving from one state to another, be sure to check the guaranty association coverage in your new state to make sure you're not putting your standard of living at risk.

Chapter 4 Simple Summary

- Single premium immediate fixed annuities can be helpful because they allow for a higher level of spending than would be safely sustainable from a typical portfolio of other investments.

- In exchange for this increased safety, you give up control of the money as well as the possibility of leaving the money to your heirs.

- Before buying an annuity, check the financial strength of the insurance company and make sure you're familiar with the rules and coverage limits for your state's guaranty association.

CHAPTER FIVE

How Much (and When) to Annuitize

Even if you had no desire whatsoever to leave anything to your heirs, it would still be unwise to annuitize your entire portfolio. The reason for this point of caution is that annuities cannot easily be sold. And since life tends to include a variety of sudden, unpredictable expenses, it's usually wise to keep a portion of your portfolio in more liquid assets (e.g., cash, bonds, stocks, and mutual funds) to serve as an "emergency fund."

So how much of your portfolio *should* you annuitize? In many cases, the answer is easy: You should annuitize enough of your portfolio to ensure that your income does not fall below the level below which you do not want it to fall. How, exactly, this decision plays out will naturally vary from person to person. Some people will prefer to lock in just enough income to cover their most basic necessities, thereby preserving more of their portfolio for investments with greater upside potential. Other people (specifically, those with less tolerance for risk) will prefer to lock in a higher level of income, even if doing so rules out the possibility of super-good outcomes that can potentially come from other investments. In addition, as we'll see shortly, some people will prefer to annuitize immediately upon retirement to get their desired level of income locked in as soon as possible, while others will prefer to take their chances with other investments, and simply use annuitization as a backup plan.

EXAMPLE: George and Sharon are ages 70 and 71, respectively. Between them, they receive a total of $19,000 per year of Social Security benefits. Neither one has any pension income. George and Sharon are very risk-averse and want to be *as sure as possible* that their total income does not fall below $35,000 per year.

If their portfolio is large enough to purchase a joint lifetime annuity paying $16,000 of inflation-adjusted income per year (that is, $35,000 of desired income, minus $19,000 of Social Security benefits) while still having enough money left over to serve as an emergency fund, it would probably be a good idea to go ahead and purchase such an annuity in order to protect their income and achieve the peace of mind they desire.

If their portfolio is *not* big enough to fund such a purchase, they're in a tough situation, with the best answer probably involving one or more of the sacrifices discussed in Chapter 3 such as cutting back on spending or finding an additional (non-portfolio) source of income.

EXAMPLE: Jennifer recently retired at age 63. She has a pension that pays $26,000 per year, and she receives Social Security of $14,000 per year. She feels that all of her most important needs can be satisfied with a $40,000 annual income. Conclusion: Jennifer has no need to annuitize any part of her portfolio.

Annuitizing as a Backup Plan

For retirees with a sufficiently large portfolio and a high risk tolerance (or a strong desire to leave behind as much money as possible to heirs), it sometimes makes sense for annuitization to be "plan B" rather than "plan A." That is:

- Begin retirement with the conventional strategy of taking periodic withdrawals from a conventional stock/bond portfolio.
- Keep an eye on how your portfolio value compares to the amount needed to purchase an annuity that would pay the desired level of income for the rest of your life.
- Then, if things go poorly and your portfolio falls to the point where it can just barely fund the purchase of such an annuity (while still having an emergency fund left over), you can

buy the annuity at that point in order to prevent things from getting any worse.

The upside of such a strategy is that it gives you the chance to experience a higher level of income (and/or leave behind a larger sum to your heirs) if your portfolio performs well. In addition, it leaves more to your heirs if you die early.

EXAMPLE: Claire is 65 years old. She wants to be sure that her income does not fall below $35,000 per year, but she is also interested in leaving some money to her two adult children when she dies.

Claire receives $18,000 of Social Security per year. She has no pension. In other words, Claire wants her portfolio to satisfy at least $17,000 of spending per year.

As I write this, the highest quote for an inflation-adjusted lifetime annuity for a single 65-year-old female is 4.36%. In other words, it would take $389,908 for Claire to be able to lock in $17,000 of annual inflation-adjusted income with an annuity (thereby giving her the $35,000 total she desires).

If Claire's portfolio is, say, $600,000, she has no need to annuitize anything right this minute. In fact there's a good chance she'll never have to annuitize anything at all. She can invest in a standard stock/bond retirement portfolio and use a conventional periodic-withdrawal strategy. If Claire's portfolio performs poorly and declines to the point at which she has just enough to lock in her desired level of spending while having an emergency fund left over, she can annuitize at that time.

Annuitization as a Backup Plan: Important Caveats

The strategy of using annuitization as a backup plan comes with some important caveats. First, it requires that you keep a close eye on things. Not only do you have to watch your portfolio, you also have to regularly get new quotes for annuities. Otherwise, if interest rates decline and you fail to notice, you could find yourself in a situation in which your portfolio is no longer sufficient to safely provide the desired level of income.

Second, it's worth noting that the psychological difficulty in putting such a backup plan into action, should it become necessary, is likely to be immense. If you're the type who finds annuitizing to be an undesirable idea even when you'd have a decent-sized portfolio left over, it's going to feel even less desirable when:

1. The necessary annuity will consume most of your net worth, and
2. Buying such an annuity will require selling your existing holdings immediately *after* a market decline.

Social Security as an Annuity

While Social Security claiming strategies are beyond the scope of this book, it's worth briefly pointing out that holding off on claiming Social Security is akin to buying an inflation-adjusted lifetime annuity—one with less credit risk *and* a higher payout than you can get from a private insurance company.

EXAMPLE: Judy just retired at age 65. Based on her earnings history, if she claims her Social Security retirement benefit right now, she would receive $16,800 per year. If she instead waits one year (thereby giving up $16,800 of benefits over the course of the year) and claims at age 66, she will receive $18,000 per year.

This is economically the same as spending $16,800 on an inflation-adjusted lifetime annuity that pays $1,200 per year (i.e., the difference between $18,000 and $16,800). That works out to a 7.14% payout rate. That's *significantly* higher than the payout rate a 66 year-old female could typically get from a private insurance company, especially when interest rates are low. (For example, as of this writing, the highest available payout showing on immediateannuities.com for a 66-year-old female is 4.51%.)

And a similar sort of analysis applies for delaying Social Security benefits all the way to age 70. The takeaway: If Judy wants to annuitize part of her portfolio in order to increase her level of safe income, holding off on claiming Social Security is likely the best way to do so.

Chapter 5 Simple Summary

- It's almost never a good idea to annuitize your entire portfolio, because doing so would leave you without a liquid "emergency fund" for dealing with large, unpredictable expenses.

- Generally speaking, the more risk-averse you are, the more of your portfolio you will want to annuitize and the sooner you will want to do so.

- Delaying Social Security is economically equivalent to buying an inflation-adjusted lifetime annuity—one that has a higher pay-out rate than you could get from an annuity purchased from an insurance company. Therefore, if you want to annuitize a part of your portfolio, you should start by considering the option to delay claiming your Social Security benefits.

PART TWO

Managing a Retirement-Stage Portfolio

By this point, we've discussed how much money you need to save in order to retire and the role annuities can play in (safely) increasing the amount of income that your portfolio provides. In this next section, we'll discuss strategies for managing the *non*-annuitized portion of your portfolio so as to minimize the risk of outliving your money.

CHAPTER SIX

Asset Allocation for Retirement Portfolios

One thing that does not change as you approach and enter retirement is the fact that your ideal asset allocation is a function of your risk tolerance. What might change, however, is your risk tolerance itself.

Assessing Your Risk Tolerance

Your risk tolerance is determined by two things:

1. How much volatility you can handle without experiencing financial problems, and
2. How much volatility you can handle without experiencing significant psychological distress.

Many investors find that both of these factors change (in favor of having less risk in the portfolio) as they get closer to retirement.

EXAMPLE: At the beginning of 2008, Phil was 60 years old and hoping to retire in the near future. During the 2008-2009 bear market, Phil's portfolio declined by roughly 30%. Phil had experienced similar percentage declines before, but this one was different for two reasons.

First, prior to the bear market, Phil's portfolio was far larger than it had been at the beginning of prior bear markets. As a result, the sheer magnitude of this decline (when measured in dollars rather than as a percentage) made this loss feel worse than prior ones. Seeing his net worth drop by an amount greater than twice his annual income was not easy.

Second, this loss had a direct impact on his life. In prior bear markets, he saw his portfolio value decline, but it didn't really change his plans in any way. This time, the decline meant that Phil had to put off retirement for another several years.

Conclusion: If you are nearing retirement, it's likely that both your psychological risk tolerance and financial risk tolerance are lower than they have been in the past.

And many investors find that their risk tolerance declines even further once they actually do retire. When you're still working, the appropriate response to a market decline is usually just to refrain from panicking and selling. Once you're retired, however, that's not always an option. You need cash to pay your bills, and if it has to come from your investments, it has to come from your investments—no matter how poorly they've performed recently.

An important point to note here is that the higher your level of safe income (e.g. Social Security, pensions, and lifetime annuities) relative to your expenses, the greater ability you will have to take risk in your portfolio. In fact, if your basic needs are entirely satisfied via safe sources of income, you may find that your risk tolerance is roughly the same as it was during your working years, because you are not relying on your portfolio for immediate income.

Asset Allocation: No "Right" Answer

When it comes to asset allocation, it can be helpful to think of a portfolio as having several levers that you can adjust upward or downward in order to increase or decrease the level of risk.

- There's a lever for adjusting the stocks-vs-bonds-vs-cash allocation,
- There are levers for adjusting the riskiness of the bonds in your portfolio, and
- There are levers for adjusting the riskiness of the stocks in your portfolio.

Because we cannot predict the future, there is no one single way to perfectly position each of those levers—no perfect asset allocation. Instead, there's a whole spectrum of *satisfactory* allocations, which can be achieved by adjusting those levers in various ways so that the resulting portfolio has an overall risk level that is appropriate for your personal risk tolerance.

Stock vs. Bond vs. Cash Lever

When choosing how much to keep in stocks (as opposed to safer things such as bonds, CDs, or cash), one common approach is to base your allocation on how much of a portfolio decline you can handle—both mentally and financially. My rule of thumb is to assume that stocks can lose 50% of their value at any time, without coming roaring back immediately. But if you want to be more conservative, you can plan for a worse scenario.[1]

EXAMPLE: Peter and Pamela are both age 70 and retired. Between their Social Security and annuity income, their basic needs are satisfied. As a result, their *financial* risk tolerance is quite high. That is, they can afford to take on a great deal of risk with the remainder of their portfolio.

---

[1] For a record of historical market declines, search online for the paper "The History and Economics of Stock Market Crashes," by Paul Kaplan et al.

But, having been through several bear markets, Peter knows that he becomes slightly irritable when their portfolio is performing poorly. And Pamela knows that "slightly irritable" is an understatement. In other words, their *psychological* risk tolerance is rather low.

After talking it over, they decide that a 20% drop in their portfolio value is the most that they can tolerate. As a result, they choose to limit their stock allocation to 40% of their portfolio.

Bond Risk Lever: Credit Quality

Bonds with more credit risk (i.e., a higher risk of default) have higher yields than bonds with less credit risk. Some experts recommend sticking exclusively to Treasury bonds, which have almost no credit risk, while other experts recommend a sizeable allocation to corporate bonds (and sometimes even high-yield "junk" bonds) as well. Either approach is perfectly reasonable. The point is simply that, *if* you choose to take on significant credit risk with your bonds, it's important to adjust your portfolio's overall risk level in other ways to ensure that it's still in line with your risk tolerance.

Bond Risk Lever: Bond Duration

Long-term bonds have higher yields than short-term bonds. They also, however, have more risk.

When interest rates rise, a bond's price will fall by an amount approximately equal to the change in the applicable interest rate, multiplied by the duration of the bond. And the opposite effect occurs when interest rates fall. For example, if a bond has a duration of 9 years, and interest rates for similar bonds increase by 1%, the bond's price will fall by approximately 9%. Conversely, if interest rates fell by 1%, the bond's price would increase by approximately 9%. This type of volatility is known as "interest rate risk."

And the same goes for bond funds: The average duration of the fund tells you how sensitive the fund will be to changes in interest rates. For example, a long-term Treasury fund with an average duration of 15 years will exhibit *far* more price volatility than a short-term Treasury fund with an average duration of just 2 years.

One strategy for dealing with interest rate risk is to use FDIC-insured CDs rather than bonds for a portion of your fixed income holdings. If you want to get rid of a bond prior to maturity, you have to sell it on the open market—at whatever the bond's market value happens to be at the time. CDs, in contrast, can be redeemed directly with the issuer. As a result, if you can find longer-term CDs with low penalties for early redemption, you can get the higher yield that comes with a longer maturity, while still having an inexpensive "out" in case you need the money before the CD matures or in case interest rates go up and you want to switch to a newer CD with a higher yield.

As with the credit-quality decision, there's no one "right" amount of interest rate risk to take on. Just be sure that *if* you decide to take on significant interest rate risk, you take other steps to ensure that the overall level of risk in your portfolio is not higher than you can tolerate.

Bond Risk Lever: Inflation-Adjusted Bonds vs. Nominal Bonds

Treasury Inflation-Protected Securities (TIPS) and Series I savings bonds ("I Bonds") are U.S. government bonds that provide a specific *after*-inflation return, in contrast to traditional "nominal" bonds that provide a specific before-inflation return. TIPS and I Bonds can be particularly useful for investors who are especially concerned about inflation risk.

EXAMPLE: Thomas is a retiree who has a government pension instead of Social Security. While his pension has a provision for inflation adjustments, the annual adjustment is limited to 2%. As a result, Thomas is more exposed to inflation risk than other retirees whose Social Security inflation adjustment has no cap. And as a retiree in general, he's more exposed to inflation risk than working investors. As such, Thomas decides to keep the inflation risk in his portfolio low by using inflation-adjusted bonds and using his other levers to achieve the desired level of overall risk and expected return.

Stock Risk Levers: Small-Cap Risk and Value Risk

Small-cap stocks are generally considered to have higher risk and higher expected returns than large-cap stocks. And value stocks (which are often stocks of distressed companies or companies in stagnant or struggling industries) are generally considered to have higher risk and higher expected returns than growth stocks.

Some investors like to have an extra allocation of small-cap/value stocks in their portfolio. That's a perfectly reasonable thing to do, but again it is important to be sure that the overall risk level of your portfolio is appropriate. (So if you choose to overweight small-cap/value stocks, you may, for example, want to prioritize using very low-risk bonds for your bond allocation. Or you may want to increase your overall bond allocation.)

Stock Risk Lever: International vs. Domestic

The United States stock market makes up approximately half of the value of world stock markets.[1] Therefore, if you had no reason to prefer domestic stocks to international stocks (or vice versa), it would be reasonable to allocate approximately half of your stock portfolio to U.S. stocks.

As a retiree living in the U.S., however, you do have a reason to prefer U.S. stocks. That reason is known as "currency risk." Currency risk is the risk that your return from international stocks will be reduced as a result of the U.S. dollar increasing in value relative to the value of the currencies of the countries in which you have invested.

EXAMPLE: A portion of your portfolio is invested in Brazilian stocks, and over the next ten years those stocks earn an annual return of 8%. However, over that same period, the Brazilian currency decreases in value relative to the dollar at a rate of 3% per year. When measured in U.S. dollars, your annual return would only be (approximately) 5%.

In other words, international stocks have an additional source of volatility: fluctuations in exchange rates. As we've discussed, volatility is *not a good thing* for a retirement portfolio. As such, it likely

---

[1] World markets as represented by the MSCI AC World Index.

44

makes sense to use U.S. stocks for the majority (though not all) of your stock portfolio.

Rebalancing Your Portfolio

Rebalancing is the process of adjusting your holdings to bring them back to your target asset allocation. Rebalancing is important because it prevents the risk level of your portfolio from drifting too far from where you want it to be.

Some experts advocate for rebalancing on a fixed schedule (e.g., on your birthday every year). Others advocate for checking your portfolio regularly and rebalancing any time it is off-target by more than a given percentage. As with other asset allocation-related decisions, we cannot know the very best approach without being able to predict the future. But whichever strategy you choose, it is important to stick with it, so that your asset allocation never gets too far out of whack.

If your portfolio includes both taxable brokerage accounts and tax-sheltered retirement accounts, it is often advantageous to rebalance by making transactions in your retirement accounts rather than in your taxable accounts, so as to defer paying taxes on capital gains.

Chapter 6 Simple Summary

- We can use historical data to make educated guesses, but there's no obviously-best asset allocation.

- When it comes to asset allocation, the most important thing you can do is simply be sure that your portfolio's overall risk level is appropriate for your risk tolerance.

- Your risk tolerance is a function of how much volatility (or how great of a loss) you can handle—both financially and psychologically.

- The risk level of your portfolio can be adjusted by changing the portion of your portfolio allocated to stocks, by changing the riskiness of the stocks in your portfolio, or by changing the riskiness of the bonds in your portfolio.

CHAPTER SEVEN

Index Funds and ETFs

Index funds are mutual funds designed to track a specific index (the S&P 500, for instance). This is in contrast to most mutual funds, which are run by fund managers seeking to *beat* a given index (i.e., earn above average returns) rather than just *match* it.[1]

Because index funds seek only to mimic an index, they can be run for significantly lower costs than other, actively managed mutual funds. For example, the typical actively managed mutual fund carries an expense ratio of roughly 0.75%, whereas it's easy to find index funds charging 0.1% or less.

Study after study has shown that low-cost mutual funds tend to outperform high-cost funds. For example, a Morningstar study found that, for the five-year period ending 12/31/2015, the

---

[1] An index is simply a number that tracks the price of certain investments. The S&P 500, for instance, tracks the price of 500 large U.S. companies.

cheapest quintile of funds outperformed the most expensive quintile of funds in every single asset class.[1] This shouldn't be any surprise, really. The less a fund charges, the more returns there are for fund investors to take home.

An additional advantage of index funds is that many of them are very broadly diversified. For example:

- An index fund tracking the Wilshire 5000 Total Market Index would own thousands of U.S. companies,
- An index fund tracking the FTSE Global All Cap ex US Index would own thousands of international companies, and
- An index fund tracking the Bloomberg Barclay's U.S. Aggregate Bond Index would own thousands of different bonds from a wide variety of borrowers.

In other words, by buying just three index funds, you could have a portfolio consisting of several thousand companies from across the globe, as well as a broadly diversified collection of bonds.

---

[1] The title of the study was "Predictive Power of Fees: Why Mutual Fund Fees Are So Important." As of this writing, you can find the study on Morningstar's website at:
http://corporate1.morningstar.com/ResearchArticle.aspx?documentId=752589

One final benefit of index funds is that they have very little "management risk." That is, you don't have to worry that your superstar fund manager will quit to go to a different firm or that your fund manager will place a large, unlucky bet on a particular stock (or industry, or country) and that you won't find out about it until it's too late.

Exchange Traded Funds (ETFs)

ETFs are essentially index funds that are bought and sold like regular stocks rather than like mutual funds.[1] Among other things (most of which aren't terribly important for the typical long-term investor), the fact that ETFs trade like stocks means that ETFs can be purchased via any brokerage firm, whereas many index funds must be purchased via an account with the company that runs the fund (unless you want to pay a commission on every purchase).

Because ETFs trade like stocks, buying or selling them has traditionally involved paying a commission to your brokerage firm. Over the last several years, however, some brokerage firms such as Vanguard, Fidelity, Schwab, and TD Ameritrade

---

[1] There are also some ETFs that are more akin to actively managed mutual funds than to index funds. For the purposes of this book, however, when I say "ETF," I'm referring to ETFs that, like index funds, are low-cost and track a specific index.

have created arrangements allowing investors to buy and sell certain ETFs without paying any trade commissions.

Chapter 7 Simple Summary

- One of the most reliable ways to find top-performing funds is to look for funds with very low costs.

- Because of their low costs, broad diversification, and transparency, index funds and ETFs are excellent tools for constructing a buy and hold portfolio.

- Unless your brokerage firm offers commission-free ETF trades, you may want to stick with traditional index funds if you expect to be making frequent transactions, such as liquidating a portion of your holdings each month.

CHAPTER EIGHT

401(k) Rollovers

After leaving your job, you'll have to decide whether or not you want to roll your 401(k) into an IRA. In most cases, the answer will be that, yes, it's preferable to roll over your 401(k).[1]

Better Investment Options in an IRA

There's no question that reducing your investment costs is one of the most reliable ways to improve your investment returns. Unfortunately, many 401(k) plans have only one low-cost investment option: an S&P 500 index fund. (And some plans don't even have that!) This can force you to either:

---

[1] I use the term 401(k) throughout this chapter, though a very similar analysis would apply to a different employer-sponsored retirement plan, such as a 403(b) or 457(b).

- Use high-cost mutual funds for the remaining portions of your portfolio (bonds, international stocks, small cap stocks, etc.), or
- Keep an inappropriately large holding of the S&P 500 index fund in order to keep costs down (thereby throwing your asset allocation out of whack).[1]

In contrast, with an IRA, you'll have access to a wide array of low-cost investment options in every asset class.

Lower Fees in an IRA

In addition to potentially limiting you to high-cost funds, some 401(k) plans include administrative fees, whereas it's easy to find brokerage firms that will charge no annual IRA fees at all.

Between less expensive investment options and lower administrative costs, it's likely that you can reduce your total investment costs by 0.5%-0.75% per year simply by moving your money from a 401(k) to an IRA. That might not sound like much, but when compounded over your whole retirement, improving your investment return by

---

[1] Some employer-sponsored plans do in fact offer a satisfactory lineup of low-cost choices. For example, federal employees with access to the Thrift Savings Plan can build an *extremely* low-cost diversified portfolio without needing to take their money anywhere else.

0.5% can have a significant impact on how long your money lasts.

Roth 401(k) Rollover to Avoid RMDs

If you have a Roth 401(k) account, there is an additional point in favor of rolling it over (into a Roth IRA). Specifically, after you reach age 70½, you will have to start taking required minimum distributions each year from your Roth 401(k). In contrast, Roth IRAs do not have required distributions while the owner is still alive. So by rolling your Roth 401(k) to a Roth IRA, you can avoid having to deal with RMDs during your lifetime.

Reasons *Not* to Roll Over a 401(k)

There are, however, a few specific situations in which it doesn't make sense to roll over a 401(k)—or other employer-sponsored retirement plan—after leaving your job.

If you are "separated from service" (i.e., you leave your job, were laid off, etc.) in a calendar year in which you turn age 55 or older, distributions from your 401(k) with that employer will not be subject to the 10% additional tax that normally comes with retirement account distributions before age 59½.

As a result, if you are 55 or older when you leave your job (or you will turn 55 later that year) and you plan to retire prior to age 59½, it may make sense to put off rolling your 401(k) into an IRA until you *are* 59½. This way, if you need to spend some of the money prior to age 59½, you can do so without having to worry about the 10% additional tax.

Alternatively, if you currently have a traditional IRA to which you made nondeductible contributions and you are planning a Roth conversion, you may want to hold off on rolling over your 401(k) until the year after you've executed the Roth conversion, so as to minimize the portion of the conversion that's taxable.[1]

Lastly, if your 401(k) includes employer stock that has significantly appreciated in value from the time you purchased it, you'd do well to speak with an accountant before rolling over your 401(k) or taking distributions from the account. Why? Because under the "net unrealized appreciation" rules, you may be able to take a lump-sum distribution of your 401(k) account, moving the employer stock into a taxable account and rolling the rest of the account into an IRA.

Why would such a maneuver be beneficial? Because, if you roll the stock into a taxable account, only your basis in the stock (i.e., the amount you paid for it) will be taxed as a distribution. The amount by which the shares have appreciated in value (the "net unrealized appreciation") isn't taxed until you sell the stock. And even then, it will be taxed at long-term capital gain tax rates (currently,

---

[1] Roth conversions are the subject of Chapter 9, so don't worry if this doesn't make much sense right now.

a max of 20%) instead of being taxed as ordinary income.[1]

In contrast, if you roll the stock into an IRA, when you withdraw the money from the IRA, the entire amount will count as ordinary income and will be taxed according to your ordinary income tax rate at the time of withdrawal.

EXAMPLE: Martha recently retired from her job with a utility company. She owns employer stock in her 401(k). The stock is currently worth $100,000. Her total cost basis for the shares is $42,000.

If she rolls her entire 401(k) into an IRA, when she withdraws that $100,000, the entire amount will be taxable as ordinary income.

If, however, she rolls the employer stock into a taxable account, she'll only be taxed upon her basis in the shares ($42,000).[2] And when she eventually sells the shares, the gain will be taxed as a long-term capital gain (at a maximum rate of 20%) rather than as ordinary income.

Remember, though, that holding a significant amount of your net worth in one company's stock is

---

[1] If the stock is sold within one year of the date of the distribution, any gain attributable to an increase in the price of the stock since the date of the distribution will be taxed as a short-term capital gain.

[2] If Martha is under age 55, it's possible that this $42,000 distribution will be subject to a 10% penalty as well as ordinary income tax. See IRS Publication 575 for details: irs.gov/publications/p575/

risky—*especially when that company is your em-ployer*. Be careful not to take on too much risk in your 401(k) solely in the hope of getting a tax ben-efit in the future.

And to reiterate, if you think you might ben-efit from the net unrealized appreciation rules, it's definitely a good idea to speak with a tax profes-sional to ensure that you execute the procedure properly.

How to Roll Over a 401(k)

In most cases, rolling over a 401(k) is just four easy steps:

1. Open a traditional IRA if you don't already have one,
2. Request rollover paperwork from your plan administrator,
3. Fill out the paperwork and send it back in, and
4. Once the money has arrived in your IRA, go ahead and invest it as you see fit.

When you're filling out the paperwork, you'll want to initiate a "direct rollover." That is, do not have the check made out to you. Have it made out to— and sent to—the new brokerage firm.

If for some reason the check arrives in your own mailbox, don't panic. But be sure to forward the check to the new brokerage firm ASAP. If you don't get it rolled over into your new IRA within 60 days, the entire amount will count as a taxable distribution this year, which would likely result in a hefty tax bill.

Where to Roll Over Your 401(k)

In terms of where to roll over your 401(k), you have three major options. You can roll your 401(k) account into an IRA at:

1. A mutual fund company,
2. A discount brokerage firm, or
3. A full service brokerage firm.

Rolling a 401(k) into an IRA with a mutual fund company can be a good choice. As long as you make sure to choose a fund company that has low-cost funds, low (or no) administrative fees for IRAs, and a broad enough selection of funds to build a diversified portfolio, you should do just fine. For example, Vanguard and Fidelity have excellent index funds and would be great places to roll over a 401(k).

Your second option is to roll your 401(k) account into an IRA at a discount brokerage firm, such as Charles Schwab. Due to the proliferation of exchange-traded funds (ETFs), you can now quickly and easily create a low-cost, diversified portfolio at any discount brokerage firm.[1]

Option #3—using a full service brokerage firm (e.g., Edward Jones)—is one I'd generally recommend against. At these companies, financial advisors will usually try to sell you a portfolio of funds with front-end commissions (a needless cost) or an advisory account with unnecessarily high ongoing fees.[2]

---

[1] And, as mentioned in the previous chapter, Schwab, Fidelity, Vanguard, and TD Ameritrade now offer commission-free trades on certain ETFs.

[2] The same thing goes for rolling a 401(k) into an IRA with an insurance company or a bank. In most cases, you'll be working with a commission-paid salesperson whose job is to sell you high-cost investments.

Chapter 8 Simple Summary

- In most cases, it's beneficial to roll your 401(k) into an IRA after leaving your job. Doing so will usually give you access to better investment options and will likely reduce your administrative costs as well.

- If you left your job at age 55 or older (or in the year in which you turn age 55), and you plan to retire prior to age 59½, you may want to postpone rolling over your 401(k) until you reach age 59½.

- If you're planning a Roth conversion of non-deductible IRA contributions, you may want to hold off on a 401(k) rollover until the year after your Roth conversion.

- If you have employer stock in your 401(k), before rolling your 401(k) into an IRA, it's probably a good idea to speak with an accountant to see if you can take advantage of the net unrealized appreciation rules.

- In most cases, the best place to roll over a 401(k) is a mutual fund company with low-cost funds or a discount brokerage firm that offers low-cost (or no-cost) trades on ETFs.

PART THREE

Tax Planning in Retirement

Tax planning for your portfolio is a critical part of a retirement plan. Every dollar of your investment returns that goes to taxes is a dollar that you don't get to spend.

As a quick refresher before we get started discussing tax planning strategies, the following page has a table comparing the three main categories of investment accounts. Please recognize, however, that:

- There are exceptions to the information provided in the table, and
- The table assumes that you've already met the various rules for taking IRA distributions without penalty.

Categories of Investment Accounts		
Type	Examples	Tax Treatment
Taxable	Taxable brokerage account	Interest is taxed at your ordinary income tax rate. Short-term capital gains are taxed at your ordinary income tax rate. Qualified dividends and long-term capital gains are taxed at a maximum rate of 20%. (And if your taxable income is low enough, they're not taxed at all.)
Tax-deferred	Traditional IRA, 401(k), 403(b), 457(b)	Money contributed to the account (usually) reduces your taxable income in the year of the contribution. Money in the account is not taxed as it grows. Instead, when you take it out of the account, it's (usually) all taxable as ordinary income.
Roth	Roth IRA, Roth 401(k), Roth 403(b)	Money in the account is neither taxed as it grows, nor when you take it out of the account (because it was taxed before you put it in).

CHAPTER NINE

Roth Conversions

A Roth conversion is a process through which you move money *from* a tax-deferred account (such as a traditional IRA) *to* a Roth account (such as a Roth IRA). The amount "converted" is taxable as income in the year of the conversion.[1] In exchange, when you withdraw the money from your Roth, it comes out tax-free.[2]

The typical motivation behind a Roth conversion is that it can lower your overall tax bill if you have a lower marginal tax rate when you execute the

---

[1] If the conversion includes amounts that were nondeductible when contributed to the tax-deferred account, the conversion may be partially or entirely nontaxable.

[2] If you take the money out prior to the first day of the fifth year after the date of the conversion, *and* you're under age 59½ when you take the distribution, it may be subject to a 10% penalty. See IRS Publication 590-B for more details: irs.gov/publications/p590b/

conversion than you expect to have later (when you take the money out of your Roth).

In case you aren't familiar with the term, your "marginal tax rate" is the rate of tax that you would pay on your next dollar of income. In most cases, your marginal tax rate is simply your federal tax bracket plus your state tax bracket. In some cases, however, your marginal tax rate can be different from just your tax bracket. For instance, if your circumstances are such that additional income would not only cause the normal amount of income tax but would also cause you to lose eligibility for a given deduction or credit, your marginal tax rate would be greater than just your tax bracket.[1]

To reiterate: The fact that you *can* convert to a Roth doesn't mean you *should.* In most cases, a Roth conversion only makes sense if you expect to have a higher marginal tax rate later than you have at the moment. As you can imagine, this is not the case for most taxpayers immediately before retirement, as most taxpayers are in a *lower* tax bracket in retirement than they were in while they were working.

---

[1] For example, if you retire prior to Medicare eligibility and you purchase health insurance on one of the exchanges created by the Affordable Care Act, additional income might not only cause the normal amount of income tax, it could also decrease the amount of the Premium Tax Credit for which you are eligible.

What Does This Have to Do With Retirement Planning?

Given the fact that you can do a Roth conversion at any age, you may wonder why I bring it up in a book about retirement planning. There are two reasons.

First, as we'll see in the next chapter, you have more control over your tax bracket from year to year during retirement than you do while you're working. This flexibility can give you more opportunities to benefit from a well-planned Roth conversion.

The second reason has to do with reaching age 59½. Specifically, prior to age 59½, it's generally unwise to execute a Roth conversion unless you have cash on hand to pay the tax on the conversion. If you use money from the IRA to pay the tax, that money will count as a distribution from your IRA. And, unless you meet one of a few exceptions, it will count as a "nonqualified distribution" from your IRA, and will be subject to a 10% penalty.[1] Once you reach age 59½, distributions aren't subject to the 10% penalty, so the amount of cash you have on hand is no longer a concern.

EXAMPLE: Claire is 50 years old and single. She has decided that she wants to convert $20,000 from her traditional IRA to her Roth IRA. Not counting the conversion, her taxable income for the year is

---

[1] You can find explanations of the potential exceptions in IRS Publication 590-B.

$60,000, putting her in the 22% tax bracket. Claire does not have any cash available with which to pay the tax on the conversion.

Claire takes $20,000 out of her traditional IRA, moves $15,600 immediately into her Roth, and saves the remaining $4,400 in a taxable account to pay the (22%) income tax that will result from taking $20,000 out of her traditional IRA. Unfortunately, because she's not yet 59½, the $4,400 that does not make it into her Roth will count as a nonqualified distribution and will be subject to a 10% ($440) penalty.

If Claire were, for instance, 60 years old instead of 50 years old, she would have been able to avoid the 10% penalty.

Takeaway: Once you're retired and you've reached age 59½, you're more likely to be able to use Roth conversions for potential tax savings.

How to Execute a Roth Conversion

The best method for executing a Roth conversion is to do a direct transfer via your fund company or brokerage firm—either online or by calling them on the phone so they can walk you through the process.

You *can* do it yourself by withdrawing the funds from your traditional IRA, then depositing them in your Roth. But this exposes you to potential errors. Specifically, if everyday life distracts you, and you don't get the funds deposited into your

Roth within 60 days, they'll no longer be eligible for conversion.

Roth Conversions of Nondeductible Contributions

If your traditional IRA includes contributions that were not deductible when you made them (because your income was too high), the portion of your Roth conversion that is attributable to nondeductible contributions will not be taxable as income. This nontaxable portion of the conversion is calculated as:

$$\text{Nondeductible contributions} \div \left(\begin{array}{c} \text{Traditional} \\ \text{IRA balance} \\ \textbf{as of 12/31} \end{array} + \begin{array}{c} \text{Distributions} \\ \text{\& conversions} \\ \text{made during} \\ \text{the year} \end{array} \right)$$

EXAMPLE: For the last 5 years, Lawrence has been making nondeductible contributions to his traditional IRA of $5,000 per year, for a total of $25,000. In June, Lawrence makes a $20,000 Roth conversion. At the end of the year, his traditional IRA is worth $55,000. One-third of his $20,000 conversion will be nontaxable, calculated as:

$25,000 ÷ ($55,000 + $20,000) = 0.33

Note: For these purposes, the IRS considers all of your traditional IRA accounts to make up one traditional IRA. So even if Lawrence's IRA was split up among several traditional IRA accounts at various brokerage firms, it would not change the calculation at all.

EXAMPLE (Part 2): Same example as above, except that Lawrence also rolls a $425,000 401(k) into his traditional IRA in August. Lawrence's rollover changes the end-of-year value of his IRA, and, therefore, the portion of his conversion that is taxable.

Specifically, Lawrence's IRA is now worth $480,000 at the end of the year. As such, only 5% of his conversion will be nontaxable, calculated as: $25,000 ÷ ($480,000 + $20,000) = 0.05.

Takeaway: If Lawrence wants to do a Roth conversion and roll over his 401(k), he may want to postpone the rollover until the year after the conversion has taken place, so as to minimize the portion of the conversion that's taxable.

Chapter 9 Simple Summary

- If you currently have a lower marginal tax rate than you expect to have later in retirement, you may be able to save money by converting your traditional IRA (or a portion of your traditional IRA) to a Roth IRA.

- While Roth conversions are helpful for any investor to understand, retirees (especially those over age 59½) have more flexibility to use them strategically.

- It's best to execute a Roth conversion directly via your brokerage firm or fund company.

- If you have made nondeductible contributions to an IRA, a portion of your Roth conversion will be nontaxable.

CHAPTER TEN

Distribution Planning

A key part of retirement planning is mini-mizing taxes by planning account distributions strategically. That is, should you take money out of your Roth IRA, traditional IRA, or taxable accounts first? Or should you be spending a little from each type of account every year?

For reasons that we'll discuss momentarily, it typically makes sense to follow a strategy roughly along these lines each year:

1. Take sufficient distributions from tax-de-ferred accounts to get full use of the standard deduction (or to get full use of your itemized deductions, if you itemize).
2. Spend next from taxable accounts (including by selling holdings, if necessary).
3a. If you expect your marginal tax rate later in retirement to be greater than your current

marginal tax rate, spend from tax-deferred accounts.

3b. Alternatively, if you expect your marginal tax rate to be lower later in retirement, spend from Roth accounts.

However, once you reach age 70½ and you have to start taking Required Minimum Distributions (RMDs), be sure to take them each year, regardless of the above strategy. The penalty on RMDs not taken by their deadline is steep enough that it outweighs other tax-saving considerations.[1]

Fill Your 0% Tax Bracket

In 2018, the standard deduction is $12,000 for single taxpayers and $24,000 for married taxpayers filing jointly. If you are age 65 or older, your standard deduction is increased by $1,600 if you are single or $1,300 if you are married filing jointly. (If both you and your spouse are age 65 or older, you standard deduction is increased by $1,300 for each of you—for a total standard deduction of $26,600.)

This standard deduction essentially gives you a sizeable 0% tax bracket. Often, the way to get the most value from this 0% tax bracket is to take distributions from tax-deferred accounts to at least

---

[1] RMDs are required for all employer-sponsored retirement accounts, as well as for traditional, SEP, and SIMPLE IRAs.

bring your income (excluding qualified dividends and long-term capital gains) up to the level of the standard deduction (or up to the amount of your itemized deductions, if you itemize).

EXAMPLE: John and Janice are mostly retired. (John has started working part-time at a local garden-supply store.) John and Janice are both 60 years old, so they're not yet receiving Social Security. Between interest income and John's wages, they earn $15,000 over the course of the year.

Due to the standard deduction, John and Janice's first $24,000 of income is free from income taxes. So it's clear that they should take at least $9,000 (that is, $24,000 minus their $15,000 of other income) from their traditional IRA because it'll be entirely tax-free.

Taxable Accounts Next

After filling your 0% tax bracket, it's often best to spend from taxable accounts before spending further from retirement accounts. The reason for doing this is that taxable accounts are generally the least tax-efficient (because you have to pay tax each year on income generated from such accounts), so it often makes sense to deplete them first.[1]

---

[1] Potential exception: If you expect to leave a large portion of your portfolio to your heirs (i.e., rather than spending it yourself during your lifetime), it *might* make

Roth or Tax-Deferred?

After spending from taxable accounts, whether to spend from tax-deferred accounts or Roth accounts will depend on your marginal tax rate. Specifically, if your current marginal tax rate is lower than your anticipated future tax rate (e.g., because you haven't yet started taking Social Security), it's usually wise to take advantage of that low current tax rate by spending from tax-deferred accounts (and possibly doing Roth conversions as well). Conversely, if your current marginal tax rate is *higher* than your anticipated future tax rate (e.g., because you are retired but your spouse has not yet retired), it's likely best to spend from Roth accounts right now, and spend from tax-deferred accounts later when you have that lower tax rate.

The following are the 2018 tax brackets for single taxpayers and married taxpayers filing jointly. They should be helpful for the following examples.

---

sense to spend from your retirement accounts before your taxable accounts in order to take advantage of the fact that your heirs would receive a "step up" in cost basis when they inherit your assets in taxable accounts. That is, when they inherit your taxable-account assets, their cost basis will be the fair market value of the assets at the time of your death.

Single (2018)

Taxable Income[1]:	The tax is:
$0 - $9,525	10% of the amount over $0
$9,526 - $38,700	$952.50 plus 12% of the amount over $9,525
$38,701 - $82,500	$4,453.50 plus 22% of the amount over $38,700
$82,501 - $157,500	$14,089.50 plus 24% of the amount over $82,500
$157,501 - $200,000	$32,089.50 plus 32% of the amount over $157,500
$200,001 - $500,000	$45,689.50 plus 35% of the amount over $200,000
$500,001+	$150,689.50 plus 37% of the amount over $500,000

---

[1] Note: "Taxable income" refers to the amount that's left after subtracting all your deductions from your total income.

Married Filing Jointly (2018)

Taxable Income:	The tax is:
$0 - $19,050	10% of the amount over $0
$19,051 - $77,400	$1,905 plus 12% of the amount over $19,050
$77,401 - $165,000	$8,907 plus 22% of the amount over $77,400
$165,001 - $315,000	$28,179 plus 24% of the amount over $165,000
$315,001 - $400,000	$64,179 plus 32% of the amount over $315,000
$400,001 - $600,000	$91,379 plus 35% of the amount over $400,000
$600,001+	$161,379 plus 37% of the amount over $600,000

EXAMPLE: Constance is single, 68 years old, and retired. She is planning to file for her Social Security benefits at age 70. She has significant savings in both a traditional IRA and a Roth IRA. She does not have a significant amount of savings in taxable accounts. Constance's annual expenses total roughly $40,000 per year.

As a single taxpayer over age 65, her first $13,600 of income is free from income tax due the standard deduction. So it makes sense for

Constance to take at least $13,600 out of her traditional IRA because it will be taxed at a rate of 0%.[1]

After that, Constance still needs to come up with another $26,400 to pay her bills. She expects her marginal tax rate to be above 10% later in retirement (due to Social Security and required minimum distributions from her traditional IRA), so it would probably be a good idea for her to take at least $9,525 out of her traditional IRA to fill up her 10% tax bracket, thereby paying tax at 10% now rather than at a higher rate later.

After accounting for the 10% tax bite, the $9,525 distribution gives Constance $8,572 to actually put toward spending, which means she still needs to satisfy another $17,828 of expenses (i.e., $26,400 − $8,572).

By the same reasoning as above, if Constance expects to have a marginal tax rate greater than 12% later in retirement, she should satisfy her remaining expenses via further distributions from her traditional IRA, paying tax at a 12% rate now rather than at a higher rate later.

In fact, if Constance expects to have a marginal tax rate greater than 12% later in retirement, after taking sufficient distributions from her traditional IRA to satisfy her current spending needs,

---

[1] This is somewhat of an oversimplification, as it assumes that Constance qualifies for no other deductions or credits whatsoever. If she does, she should take more out of her traditional IRA.

she should go ahead and do a Roth conversion to fill up the 12% tax bracket.

And if she expects a marginal tax rate of greater than 22% later in retirement, she should even do Roth conversions to fill her 22% bracket as well.

What about an investor who expects to be in a *lower* tax bracket later? In that case, it's best to refrain from taking traditional IRA distributions. Instead, save the traditional IRA balance so that you can take distributions later, once you're in that lower tax bracket. In the meantime, spend first from taxable accounts, then from a Roth IRA if necessary.

EXAMPLE: Raymond and Louisa are 60 years old. Raymond is retired, but Louisa doesn't plan to retire for a few more years. Louisa earns $50,000 this year, which is just shy of their $55,000 annual living expenses.

Louisa's income puts them in the 12% tax bracket. Once Louisa retires, they expect to be in the 10% tax bracket. As a result, it doesn't make sense to fund their remaining expenses with traditional IRA distributions (paying tax at a 12% rate) when they could wait and pay tax at a 10% rate later. Louisa and Raymond decide, therefore, to use some of their Roth IRA assets to fund their remaining expenses this year.

Social Security: It's Complicated.

Once an investor begins receiving Social Security benefits, things become even more complicated.

The complicating factor is that, as your income proceeds through a certain range, the portion of your Social Security income that is subject to income tax increases as well. This can lead to circumstances in which, for example, despite being in the 12% tax bracket, your marginal tax rate is actually significantly higher than 12%, because, in addition to each additional dollar of income being taxed at 12%, each additional dollar of income also causes 50 or 85 cents of Social Security income to become taxable as well.

The same general process as described earlier in this chapter still applies: Take sufficient tax-deferred distributions to make full use of your standard deduction (or itemized deductions). Then spend from taxable accounts. Then take distributions from your traditional IRA if you currently have a lower marginal tax rate than you expect to have later. (Or spend from Roth accounts if you currently have a higher marginal tax rate than you expect to have later.) The only thing that changes is that it becomes significantly more complicated to determine both your current marginal tax rate and your future marginal tax rate.[1]

---

[1] For a more thorough discussion of taxation of Social Security benefits, see my book *Social Security Made Simple* or IRS Publication 915.

    As you might imagine, a financial planner with expertise in tax planning and Social Security benefits can be very helpful here. Paying for a few hours of such a professional's time could quite possibly save you several thousand dollars in taxes.

Chapter 10 Simple Summary

- Strategically planning which accounts to spend from first can reduce your overall tax burden throughout retirement.

- In general, each year, it makes sense to take sufficient distributions from tax-deferred accounts to make full use of your standard deduction or itemized deductions.

- After taking such distributions, it's usually best to spend from your taxable accounts in order to preserve your tax-advantaged retirement accounts.

- After spending from taxable accounts, take distributions from your tax-deferred accounts if you currently have a lower marginal tax rate than you expect to have later. Or spend from Roth accounts if you currently have a higher marginal tax rate than you expect to have later.

- A financial planner who is knowledgeable about tax planning and Social Security planning has the potential to save you a great deal of money.

CHAPTER ELEVEN

Asset Location

Asset location is the process of determining which investments to keep in which accounts. That is, after you've determined your appropriate asset allocation, how should you divvy up your investments between tax-sheltered accounts and taxable accounts?

EXAMPLE: Terry is 65 years old and retired. He has decided that his appropriate asset allocation is a simple 40/60 stock/bond split. He currently has $275,000 in a traditional IRA, $75,000 in a Roth IRA, and another $150,000 invested in taxable accounts.

So, Terry's grand total portfolio is $500,000, and he would like $200,000 (40%) invested in stocks and $300,000 (60%) invested in bonds.

How should Terry go about divvying up each of his accounts between stocks and bonds? The following table outlines four possible options:

	Tax-Sheltered Accounts		Taxable
	Traditional IRA	**Roth IRA**	**Account**
1	$165,000 bonds $110,000 stocks	$45,000 bonds $30,000 stocks	$90,000 bonds $60,000 stocks
2	$275,000 bonds	$25,000 bonds $50,000 stocks	$150,000 stocks
3	$150,000 bonds $125,000 stocks	$75,000 stocks	$150,000 bonds
4	$100,000 bonds $175,000 stocks	$75,000 bonds	$125,000 bonds $25,000 stocks

Most investors wouldn't put a lot of thought into the difference between the above scenarios. After all, each of them results in a portfolio that has $300,000 of bonds and $200,000 of stocks. But, as we'll see in a minute, Terry can probably save some money on taxes by choosing option #2 because it's the scenario in which all of his bonds are in tax-sheltered accounts.

Tax-Shelter Your Bonds and CDs

It's usually beneficial to tax-shelter your fixed income investments (that is, put them in an IRA or other tax-advantaged retirement account) before tax-sheltering your stocks. Why? Because stocks are typically more tax-efficient than fixed income holdings.

Interest is usually taxed as ordinary income, at whatever your marginal tax rate happens to be. In contrast, stock gains come in the form of either dividends or capital gains. Long-term capital gains (those which occur after selling an asset that was held for longer than one year) and most dividends are taxed at a lower rate than most other types of income.

Specifically, long-term capital gains and qualified dividends are taxed at a 0% rate if they fall below $38,600 of taxable income if you're single or $77,200 if you're married filing jointly. They are taxed at a 15% rate if they fall above the 0% threshold but below $425,800 of taxable income if you're single or $479,000 if you're married filing jointly. And they are taxed at a 20% rate if they fall above the 15% threshold.

EXAMPLE: Linda is single. She has $6,000 of long-term capital gains and qualified dividends in 2018. Excluding the above income, her taxable income for the year is $35,000.

Her first $3,600 of long-term capital gains and qualified dividends are untaxed, because they fall below the $38,600 threshold. The remaining $2,400 will be taxed at a 15% rate.

As a result of the advantageous tax treatment for qualified dividends and long-term capital gains, you typically stand to benefit more from tax-shel-tering your bonds than you do from tax-sheltering your stocks.

In addition to their favorable tax rates, stocks have the following tax-efficient characteristics:

- Because capital gains are not taxed until the investment is sold, stocks are already tax-deferred to some extent, and
- Because they are volatile, stocks often provide opportunities for tax-loss harvesting.[1]

The Role of Interest Rates

It's worth noting that the importance and validity of this strategy of tax-sheltering your bonds depends on the yield of your bond holdings. Specifically, the lower the yield on your bond holdings, the less you stand to gain from tax-sheltering them. For example, if you're an investor who prefers to stick to very safe bonds such as short-term Treasury bills, you

---

[1] Tax-loss harvesting is the strategy of selling investments in taxable accounts that have declined in value since you purchased them (so that you can use the capital loss to offset some of your taxable income) and replacing those investments with other similar (but not identical) investments. For a more thorough discussion of tax-loss harvesting, see:
obliviousinvestor.com/tax-loss-harvesting/

won't stand to gain much from tax-sheltering your bonds because (due to their safety and resultantly-low yields) your bonds generate very little taxable income in the first place. (This is especially true at times when interest rates are particularly low.)

Tax-Shelter Your REITs

One important exception to the general guideline of tax-sheltering bonds before stocks is that, if you own any real estate investment trusts (REITs) or REIT funds, you'll likely want to make it a priority to tax-shelter them, even though they're stocks. The reason is that a significant portion of a REIT's dividend yield is considered *non*qualified dividends, so it is taxed as ordinary income, rather than being taxed at the advantageous tax rates of qualified dividends. As a result, REITs are tax-inefficient and should be tax-sheltered if possible.

Foreign Tax Credit

After tax-sheltering your REITs and your bonds, if you have a choice between tax-sheltering your domestic stocks or your international stocks, it's generally best to tax-shelter your domestic holdings, so as to take advantage of the foreign tax credit.

What's the foreign tax credit? The IRS explains it this way: "You can claim a credit for foreign taxes that are imposed on you by a foreign country or U.S. possession." In other words, the idea of the credit is to eliminate double taxation on foreign income.

Similarly, according to IRS Publication 514, "If you are a shareholder of a mutual fund...you may be able to claim the credit based on your share of foreign income taxes paid by the fund if it chooses to pass the credit on to its shareholders."

EXAMPLE: In your taxable brokerage account, you earn $1,000 of dividend income over the course of the year from your non-U.S. stocks, and you pay $100 in foreign taxes on that income. You can claim a $100 credit for foreign taxes paid, thereby reducing your U.S. income tax by $100.[1]

It's important to note that investments held in a retirement account—like an IRA or 401(k)—do not qualify for the credit. This is why, when making asset location decisions, it's best to tax-shelter your domestic stock funds before tax-sheltering your international stock funds.

---

[1] For the details of how the foreign tax credit is calculated, see IRS publication 514, available at: irs.gov/publications/p514/

Tax-Sheltering Priority List

In summary, the typical priority for tax-sheltering investments is as follows:

1. REITS
2. Fixed income investments with a high yield
3. Fixed income investments with a low yield
4. Domestic stocks
5. International stocks

Remember: With few exceptions, even the most tax-efficient investments are better off in a tax-sheltered account than in a taxable account.[1] So if you have sufficient room in your retirement accounts to tax-shelter everything, it's generally wise to do so.

---

[1] The most notable exception being municipal bonds, which pay interest that's free from federal income tax.

Chapter 11 Simple Summary

- You can likely achieve some tax savings by making it a priority to tax-shelter your least tax-efficient assets before tax-sheltering your other assets.

- REITs are decidedly tax-inefficient. As such, they're the highest priority for tax-sheltering. High-yield bonds are also distinctly tax-inefficient.

- If you have room to tax-shelter *either* your international stocks *or* your domestic stocks, it is usually best to tax-shelter the domestic stocks, because if you tax-shelter the international stocks you will lose out on the foreign tax credit.

CHAPTER TWELVE

Other Tips for Taxable Accounts

Whether due to selling a home in order to downsize or having socked away more money per year than you could contribute to retirement accounts, it's likely that by the time you retire, you have more assets in taxable accounts than you've had at any other time in your life.

My suggestions for investing in taxable accounts can be summed up as follows:

1. Make intelligent asset location decisions, and
2. Choose tax-efficient investments whenever possible.

We covered asset location in the previous chapter, so let's take a look at how to select tax-efficient investments.

Look for Low Portfolio Turnover

A mutual fund's "portfolio turnover" refers to the portion of the assets held by the fund that were bought or sold over the course of the year. Higher turnover usually leads to higher costs in terms of commissions and bid/ask spreads. And, if you're investing in a taxable account, higher turnover usually leads to higher taxes as well.

The reason that high portfolio turnover leads to higher taxes is that the fund's capital gain distributions will be primarily short-term rather than long-term, and they will therefore be taxed at your ordinary income tax rate rather than the more favorable long-term capital gains tax rate. Higher turnover also minimizes the potential for delaying taxes on capital appreciation.

For the most part, index funds and ETFs have low portfolio turnover and are, therefore, fairly tax-efficient (relative to most actively managed funds).

Tax-Exempt Bonds

As we discussed in the previous chapter, it's often best to tax-shelter your bonds if possible. But if you do own bonds in a taxable account, you should consider using tax-exempt municipal bonds (or tax-exempt bond funds).[1] To determine whether it's advantageous to use tax-exempt bonds, compare their yield to the after-tax yield that you could get from a taxable bond fund of similar duration and credit rating.

EXAMPLE: As of this writing, the yield on Vanguard's Total Bond Market Index Fund ("Admiral shares") is 3.05%. If you're in the 24% tax bracket, this would provide an after-tax yield of 2.32%, calculated as 3.05% x 0.76. This tells you that, if a tax-exempt bond fund of similar credit rating and duration is yielding greater than 2.32%, the tax-exempt fund would be a good choice.

Note: If your state exempts its own municipal bonds from state income tax and you are evaluating a low-cost bond fund that invests exclusively in tax-exempt bonds from within your state, be sure to use your combined state and federal tax rate when determining the after-tax yield of taxable bond funds.

EXAMPLE: If you live in New Jersey and are in the 24% federal tax bracket and 6.37% state tax bracket (for a total tax rate of 30.37%), your after-tax yield on Vanguard's Total Bond Market Index Fund as of this writing would be 2.12%, calculated as 3.05% x 0.6963. As such, if you can find a low-cost fund of tax-exempt New Jersey municipal bonds that has

---

[1] Bonds issued by states and municipalities are free from federal income tax.

similar risk to the Vanguard Total Bond Market Index Fund and which has a yield greater than 2.12%, it may be a better choice.

If you're considering investing in municipal bonds, remember that they carry credit risk (that is, the risk that the bond issuer will default on the debt). This means that:

1. It's important to diversify among issuers. (Investing via a fund makes this easier.)
2. For it to make sense to invest in municipal bonds, they must offer a higher after-tax yield than Treasury bonds of a similar duration. Otherwise there's no reason to take on the additional risk.

Avoid Funds of Funds

Balanced funds and target date funds can be an excellent, hands-off way to implement an asset allocation strategy. Owning such funds in a taxable account, however, is generally not a good idea for a handful of reasons.

First, the bond portion of such funds' portfolios are typically made up of taxable bonds (or taxable bond funds). This isn't inherently bad, but if you're in one of the top tax brackets, you may be better off with tax-exempt bonds.

Second, because they include both stocks and bonds in a single fund, they get in the way of an asset location strategy. If you have assets in both taxable accounts and tax-sheltered accounts, it's best to own your bond funds and stock funds separately so that you can place them in the most advantageous accounts.

Third, with a fund of funds, you will have fewer opportunities for tax-loss harvesting than you would have with a portfolio that consists of separate funds for each asset class.[1]

Realizing Capital Gains

One final note about investing in taxable accounts: If you have a large unrealized capital gain built up in a tax-inefficient investment, it may not make sense to sell that investment in order to move your money into something more tax-efficient. You'll have to weigh the cost of paying tax on the gain now against the savings you hope to achieve in the future with a more tax-efficient alternative.

---

[1] Again, for a more thorough discussion of tax-loss harvesting, see:
obliviousinvestor.com/tax-loss-harvesting/

Chapter 12 Simple Summary

- The lower a fund's portfolio turnover, the more tax-efficient it's likely to be.

- Depending on your tax bracket and current interest rates, tax-exempt municipal bonds may offer a higher after-tax yield than taxable bonds with similar credit risk and duration. Remember, though, that they carry more credit risk than Treasury bonds, so it's important to diversify among issuers.

- "Funds of funds" (such as balanced funds or target date funds) are generally tax-inefficient for several reasons. It's often wise to avoid them when investing in a taxable account.

Getting Help with Your Plan

In my book *Investing Made Simple*, I wrote that most investors do not need a financial advisor if they're willing to take the time to learn all the ins and outs of managing a portfolio. I still believe that to be the case.

I also wrote, however, that as an investor gets closer to retirement, the usefulness of a financial planner increases dramatically. By the time you retire, your portfolio is (hopefully) quite substantial in size. Therefore, mistakes are more costly than they've ever been. And at age 60, you have fewer remaining working years to make up for mistakes than you had at age 30.

In addition, as we've seen throughout this book, the complexity involved with a retirement-stage portfolio is far greater than that of an accumulation-stage portfolio. Whoever is managing your finances (whether you or an advisor), is going to have to:

1. Create a plan for managing your portfolio such that it will provide sufficient funding to satisfy your needs over a multiple-decade retirement,
2. Determine the most advantageous order of distributions from your various accounts,
3. Determine how Roth conversions fit into that distribution plan,
4. Develop an asset location plan that will minimize your taxes while still providing sufficient liquidity,
5. Deal with a variety of non-portfolio-related financial decisions such as when to claim Social Security and whether or not it makes sense to buy long-term care insurance, and
6. Adjust all of the above as necessary to account for changes in your life or changes in tax law.

While I believe that a motivated individual with sufficient free time and math skills can certainly get the job done on his or her own, many retirees stand to benefit from a meeting (or, more likely, ongoing meetings) with an advisor.

Important Areas of Expertise

As you can see from the list above, if you decide to use the services of an advisor, you'll want to look for somebody who can do more than just set up a portfolio. You want an advisor who is truly an expert in retirement planning. Among other things, this person should be knowledgeable about:

- IRA distribution planning,
- Social Security strategies,
- The interaction between Social Security and income tax and the tax-planning opportunities that interaction creates,
- Using asset allocation to control risk,
- Using asset location to minimize taxes, and
- Using annuities to offset longevity risk and what to look for (or avoid) in an annuity.

Certain certifications can be helpful indicators of expertise. For example, somebody who is a Certified Financial Planner (CFP) is going to be knowledgeable about both taxation and investing. Alternatively, a CPA with the PFS (Personal Financial Specialist) designation is likewise going to be an expert on both taxation and investment planning.

You can find a CFP near you by visiting cfp.net/search. And you can find a local CPA with the PFS designation by visiting: aicpa.org/forthepublic/findacpa.html.

Investment Philosophy

As mentioned briefly in Chapter 3, most mutual fund managers fail to outperform their respective indexes. And these people are intelligent, full-time professionals.

You should, therefore, be wary of any financial advisor who suggests that he can reliably earn above-market returns. After all, in addition to running your portfolio and the portfolios of all his other clients, this person has to perform marketing services for his business, keep up with tax law changes, stay up to date with regulatory and compliance issues, and much more. To think that—in his remaining time—he can reliably achieve something that most full-time professionals fail to achieve is unreasonably optimistic.

Advisor Compensation

Finally, after narrowing your options down to advisors with sufficient expertise and realistic investment philosophies, you'll want to be careful to choose an advisor with a compensation structure that's a good fit for your needs. In most cases, the goal is to eliminate as many conflicts of interest as possible while still being affordable.

Commission-Paid Advisors

In most cases, I'd suggest staying away from advisors who use commission as a compensation structure. It creates too many conflicts of interest.

For example, if you use ETFs or individual stocks, a commission-paid advisor will have an incentive to convince you to move your money around more often than is beneficial, in order to collect a commission on each trade.

If you prefer traditional mutual funds, a commission-paid advisor is only going to be able to recommend funds that charge a commission (known as a sales load). This is unfortunate, because these funds are usually actively managed funds with annual operating costs several times higher than those of a low-cost index fund.

"Assets Under Management" Advisors

Many people claim that the best advisor is one who is paid as a function of your account size (i.e., your "assets under management" or "AUM"). AUM fees tie the advisor's interests to yours—or so goes the claim. What they really do is tie the advisor's interests to your *account size*, not to your overall financial well-being. For the most part, this is not a problem, but it does present a conflict of interests whenever the most appropriate thing for you to do is liquidate a part of your portfolio (for example, to pay down your mortgage, delay claiming Social Security, buy a lifetime annuity, or buy a piece of real estate).

EXAMPLE: Dennis is 70 years old. He has no children and no desire to leave any money behind when he dies. He has a $500,000 portfolio, from which he needs to withdraw $30,000 each year. In other words, Dennis is looking at a 6% withdrawal rate–higher than many people would consider safe, even for a 70-year-old.

In such a scenario, a single premium immediate annuity might make a lot of sense. But if Dennis is currently using an advisor who charges based on account size—let's say 1% of assets—the advisor stands to gain thousands of dollars *each year* by convincing Dennis *not* to buy the annuity.

Hourly or Fee-for-Service Advisors

Other advisors charge based on a simple hourly fee or a fee-for-service arrangement in which you pay a flat fee for a given service (e.g., $X for an annual portfolio checkup). Like the other methods of advisor compensation, this one suffers from its own conflicts of interest. Hourly advisors need to keep you coming back year after year, so they don't have much incentive to teach you to manage your portfolio on your own (which could be a problem if that's your eventual goal). They also have somewhat of an incentive to over-plan—that is, to do more analysis on any given question than is really necessary.

That said, if I had to suggest one compensation structure for a financial planner, this is the one I would suggest, as I think it does the best job of minimizing conflicts of interest.

Take Your Time

As you might imagine, it can take time to find an advisor who has the expertise you need, an investment philosophy you believe in, and a compensation structure that minimizes conflicts of interest while still being affordable. That's OK. This is not a decision you want to rush.

My parting message for do-it-yourself investors is similar: The decisions you make with your portfolio immediately before and after retirement will have a dramatic impact on your standard of living going forward. So remember: There's no need to rush. With each decision, take your time and educate yourself fully before making any major changes.

And on that note, I'll leave you with my suggestions for further reading.

Appendix:
Suggestions for Further Reading

The Bogleheads' Guide to Retirement Planning, by Taylor Larimore, Mel Lindauer, Richard Ferri, Laura Dogu, and more

Can I Retire Yet?: How to Make the Biggest Financial Decision of the Rest of Your Life, by Darrow Kirkpatrick

The Little Book of Common Sense Investing, by John Bogle

The Four Pillars of Investing, by William Bernstein

The Little Book of Safe Money, by Jason Zweig

The New Coffeehouse Investor, by Bill Schultheis

The Only Guide You'll Ever Need to the Right Financial Plan, by Larry Swedroe

A Random Walk Down Wall Street, by Burton Malkiel

Retirement Portfolios, by Michael Zwecher

Unveiling the Retirement Myth, by Jim Otar

Acknowledgements

As always, my thanks go to my editing team: Michelle, Pat, Debbi, and Kalinda. Once again, you've impressed me with your ability to make my writing readable.

Also, my sincere gratitude goes to the following people who were kind enough to contribute their time and expertise to help catch my errors and omissions: Dylan Ross, CFP; Jim Blankenship, CFP, EA; Thomas Booker, CPA; and Taylor Larimore, esteemed Boglehead author.

Finally, thanks to you, the reader. It's a dream come true to get to do this for a living.

A Note on IRS Publications

Throughout the book, I reference a few IRS publications, as I believe that they're a helpful source of information for most taxpayers. Please note, however, that IRS publications do not have any legal authority. So, for example, if the information in an IRS publication contradicts the information in the actual Internal Revenue Code, it is the Code that wins.

Notes on Data

Stock and bond returns for the discussion in Chapter 2 come from the *2018 Stocks, Bonds, Bills, and Inflation (SBBI) Yearbook*. For stock returns, the "Large Company Stocks" data series is used, and for bond returns the "Intermediate-Term Government Bonds" data series is used.

About the Author

Mike is the author of several books as well as the popular blog ObliviousInvestor.com. He is a Missouri licensed CPA. Mike's writing has been featured in many places, including *The Wall Street Journal*, *Money*, *Forbes*, and *MarketWatch*.

Also by Mike Piper

Accounting Made Simple: Accounting Explained in 100 Pages or Less

Cost Accounting Made Simple: Cost Accounting Explained in 100 Pages or Less

Independent Contractor, Sole Proprietor, and LLC Taxes Explained in 100 Pages or Less

Investing Made Simple: Investing in Index Funds Explained in 100 Pages or Less

LLC vs. S-Corp vs. C-Corp Explained in 100 Pages or Less

Microeconomics Made Simple: Basic Microeconomic Principles Explained in 100 Pages or Less

Social Security Made Simple: Social Security Retirement Benefits Explained in 100 Pages or Less

Taxes Made Simple: Income Taxes Explained in 100 Pages or Less

INDEX

84403029R00076

Made in the USA
San Bernardino, CA
08 August 2018